AN INVESTMENT JOURNEY

YOUR PASSPORT TO FINANCIAL FREEDOM

Exploring the Science and Art of Investing

Frederick A. Wilhelm Jr.

Charleston, SC
www.PalmettoPublishing.com

AN INVESTMENT JOURNEY: Your Passport to Financial Freedom
Copyright © 2022 by Frederick A. Wilhelm Jr.

All rights reserved

No portion of this book may be reproduced, stored in a retrieval system, or transmitted in any form by any means—electronic, mechanical, photocopy, recording, or other—except for brief quotations in printed reviews, without prior permission of the author.

Paperback ISBN: 978-1-68515-929-0

ABOUT THE AUTHOR

Frederick A. Wilhelm Jr. is a graduate of the U.S. Naval Academy. After serving as a fighter pilot, he received a master's degree in computer science and holds multiple patents in computer engineering.

He led the network-interconnect design team for the precursor of the internet, the ARPAnet, working with the Defense Advanced Research Projects Agency (DARPA).

His team partnered with the biotech and pharmaceutical industries and leading university artificial Intelligence (AI) departments, applying computing to DNA analysis, gene splicing, and molecular modeling applications.

Retiring from the computer industry, Fred received the CFP certificate from the College for Financial Planning. For over 25 years, he has worked in the wealth management industry, being the former founder and CEO of Tecumseh Investment Management.

He is currently a founder and chief financial officer for the non-profit Santa Cruz Foundation for the Performing Arts.

DISCLAIMER NOTICE

The information contained within this document is for educational and entertainment purposes only. All effort has been executed to present accurate, up-to-date, reliable, complete information.

No warranties of any kind are declared or implied. Readers acknowledge that the author is not engaged in the rendering of legal, financial, medical, or professional advice. The content of this book has been derived from various sources.

Please consult a licensed professional before attempting any techniques outlined in this book.

By reading this document, the reader agrees that under no circumstances is the author responsible for any losses, direct or indirect, that are incurred as a result of the use of the information contained within this document, including, but not limited to, errors, omissions, or inaccuracies.

PREFACE

"Investing is not nearly as difficult as it looks. Successful investing involves doing a few things right and avoiding serious mistakes" - John C, Bogle

Investing is not just a science – it's a combination of science and art, but more art than science because there is so much human behavior in stock market economics. Instruments of economics are never totally predictable because human behavior isn't!

There is access to a vast amount of information today, but that doesn't mean it can be understood or made sense of. Sometimes too much information is the same as no information. Even though there are internet search engines, it's still a struggle to find only the factual information that is relevant.

My goal is to cut through the noise and provide you with the essential information and tools you will need to give you the confidence to become financially independent through investing wisely – to build a solid financial foundation that will provide you with the financial freedom to last your lifetime!

Forty years ago, the hub of the stock market was centered on the trading floors of Wall Street with lots of shouting, frantic brokers, surrounded by discarded crumpled trade tickets.

Technology and the advent of the internet have changed all that with lightning speed. The power of making money is no longer in the hands of a few.

There are unbelievable opportunities now because the investing world has seen one of the most significant evolutions in this century. Advancements in financial technology, or "Fintech," along with a general movement into online business and interaction, have made finance and investing more available to the general public and led to the democratization of financial markets.

TABLE OF CONTENTS

Introduction:	Beginning Your Investment Journey	1
Chapter 1	Fall Back Savings	3
Chapter 2	Retirement Income	6
Chapter 3	Risk	12
Chapter 4	Types Of Risks	15
Chapter 5	Building Your Portfolio	22
Chapter 6	Strategies	31
Chapter 7	Active Investing	41
Chapter 8	Passive Investing	50
Chapter 9	Diversification And Allocation	54
Chapter 10	Words To The Wise	62
Chapter 11	Your Advisor	70
Chapter 12	Your Account	75
Chapter 13	Keep It Simple	78
Chapter 14	Wisdom From The Wizards	81
Closing Chapter:	Thoughts About Your Journey	84

Appendices · · · · · 86
   Appendix A - Financial Terminology · · · · · 86
   Appendix B - Stock Analysis 101 · · · · · 87
   Appendix C - The Federal Reserve · · · · · 92
   Appendix D - Investment News And Research Sources · · · · 96

INTRODUCTION

BEGINNING YOUR INVESTMENT JOURNEY

To ensure a safe and successful long-term journey, the first thing to do is to map out your goals. Then become knowledgeable about the terrain and survival methods that may be required along the way. Now, of course, you will need sufficient provisions, which equate to money, for without money, the journey will end. Finally, you need to prepare for any eventuality and peril that may be encountered, so you must be aware of the risks associated with them and your limitations. With this in mind, you have the beginnings of planning your investment strategies for the success of your short and long-term goals.

The investment arena can be unpredictable, so be determined to learn and become a successful investor. The process of investing and fulfillment can be a long one. The market can prove you wrong, but don't give up. Instead, learn from your mistakes.

CHAPTER ONE

FALL BACK SAVINGS

Emergency Fund
The first thing you need to think of before putting money into the stock market is to make sure you have enough money to survive the market ups and downs and still feed your family? Don't forget that your investing money should be what you can afford to lose—*if you can't afford to lose it, don't invest it.*

With that being said, you need to make sure of continued financial stability during this new journey. Therefore, reduce any debt load as much as possible and ***never use credit cards to get cash for investing —a path to disaster.***

Be sure to have at least 6-12 months of emergency savings to avoid having to sell when the market turns down during significant market corrections, like the 2008 financial crisis. It's a terrible feeling to have to sell in a down market to pay for living expenses. Your fund should be liquid, so it could come into play whenever needed. ***Think of it as an insurance policy against bankruptcy.***

Once your emergency fund is secure, start thinking about your investment objectives. They will help form your strategy. In general, investing in the stock market should be approached with a long-term horizon in mind.

Start funding your investment account as early as possible, with at least 10% of your pre-tax income invested periodically. Of course, this amount should be much more if you start later in life.

Take advantage of your employer offerings -

If you're someone working at a company, you could be missing out on opportunities that can help you grow your net worth. It's essential to thoroughly review your employer's benefit options since companies may provide more than simply retirement plans—they can also assist you in saving money and investing to increase your earnings.

Check to see if your employer offers programs such as:

* Workplace retirement match

* Group life and disability insurance. Health Savings Account (some employers will match your payments up to a specific amount if you qualify for an HSA)

* Employee stock purchase plans

Have a budget - Clients who maintain a budget track their money more effectively. Not having a budget makes it hard to know where you are spending your money or difficult to have control over your spending in general. Once you know your financial situation, you can invest additional cash into the stock market.

"It's not the money — rather, it's the freedom that comes with the money."

CHAPTER TWO

RETIREMENT INCOME

What is your retirement vision? - Lifestyle is an essential consideration. For example, will you be a home-based person, or will you want to travel when you retire? Choices like these will determine how much money you will need in retirement.

Reliable income sources available during retirement are also critical to having a successful outcome.

    Retirement Plans - Do you have a pension or a contribution plan like a 401k or IRA? Take advantage of your company's contributions, and always fund your IRAs each year. Consider converting to a Roth IRA when you qualify, usually at 59 ½.

The principal difference between Roth IRAs and most other tax-advantaged plans is that rather than granting a tax reduction for contributions to the retirement plan, qualified withdrawals from the Roth IRA are tax-free, and growth in the account is also tax-free. But of course, you need to consider if you will have a lower tax rate when you retire, and so it might be better to put the maximum cash you are allowed in a traditional IRA to pay less in overall taxes in your lifetime. Your choice depends on one thing, taxes! If your current tax rate is higher than what it will be when you withdraw, then a traditional IRA is right for you. Otherwise, a Roth is the best choice.

Social Security provides a guaranteed source of income in retirement. Still, how much depends on your income during your working years and the age when you begin claiming benefits. Therefore, you must wait before claiming benefits until your full retirement age – 66 or 67, depending on your birth year if you want the total amount you are entitled to based on your work record.

Starting sooner reduces your per-check benefit. For example, if you begin right away at 62, you will receive only 70% of your scheduled benefit. By contrast, delaying benefits can mean more money over your lifetime.

For example, if you start receiving retirement benefits at age 67, you will get 108 percent of the monthly benefit because you delayed getting benefits for 12 months. At 70, you will receive 132 percent of the monthly benefit because you delayed getting benefits for 48 months.

As a result, retirees who wait to claim can get hundreds of dollars more each month than those who take benefits early. But, of course, this isn't feasible for everyone. So before making any moves, figure out the strategy that maximizes your household's total lifetime benefits.

You won't get it if you don't formally request your Social Security benefit. Social Security isn't in the business of letting you know what it owes you, never mind that you have paid FICA taxes your entire working life for those benefits. The Social Security has thousands of rules, which its staff can get wrong, so talk to multiple offices and do your research.

Bond Income - A bond is an instrument of indebtedness of the bond issuer to the holder. In return for the bond holder's money, the issuer is obligated to make periodic interest payments to the bondholder and repay the loan when the loan term ends—***more about bonds in chapter 7.***

Annuity Income - An annuity is a contract between an individual or married couple and an insurance company. You can purchase an annuity with a portion of your retirement savings in either a single payment or with multiple payments, depending on the type of annuity. Once you own an annuity, any growth in your account may be on a tax-deferred basis while you continue to have control of your money, as needed.

Annuities can ensure that your retirement income is protected even when there are downturns in the market. The downside is usually a high upfront commission and punitive cancellation fees if funds are needed before the contract is satisfied.

Retirement Savings Withdrawals - You may consider making systematic withdrawals from your total retirement funds when you retire by taking out a certain percentage in your first year and then increasing slightly every year after that to counter inflation. Conversely, you might have to decrease your withdrawal if your investments take a hit, or you may be able to bump it up if they are performing well.

Bottom Line - Once you have your income streams nailed down, you need to estimate how your retirement vision measures up.

Seamless Transition Estimate

Scenario: you plan to retire at 67 with a final income of $150,000 per year and plan on continuing that income lifestyle until a life expectancy of 85 (18 years). You will need to have retirement savings of approximately $2.7 million.

Retirement calculators are accessible online at Fidelity, Vanguard, and AARP sites. You can input factors such as present age, pre-tax income, current savings, and monthly retirement savings to get a detailed estimate on how much you will have at retirement.

For example, if you are 35 years old with a pre-tax income of $60,000 and have a retirement savings of $30,000, and are saving $500 per month for retirement at age 67, you would have $880,000. But if your life expectancy were to live to age 95, you would need $1.73M.

retirement calculation assumptions:
6% investment annual rate of return
3% inflation
2% salary increase per year

You should plan to be debt-free at retirement with no car loans or mortgages if possible. Mortgages are tax and financial losers. Pay them off ASAP. Think about it: If you have $100,000 that you can invest right now in a bond earning 1.5%, you'd have $1,500 in interest income over the course of a year. But if you had a $100,000 debt at a 3.2% interest that you could pay off right now, you'd save $3,200 over the course of the year in interest payments. On balance, you'd make $1,700 with no risk by investing in debt repayment rather than investing in the bond.

Owning a home can reduce longevity risk. Here's another reason it's better to own instead of rent. Let's say you're 70 and have found your dream location. Renting for the rest of your life runs the risk of rent hikes without the possibility of your fixed-income increasing. In contrast, home prices can soar or collapse if you own your home, but you'll be insulated. Since you are neither buying nor selling your home, who cares what the housing market does? Your housing consumption is guaranteed through the end of your days.

Home Equity Income using a reverse mortgage

Another income source could be an FHA-insured reverse mortgage if things get tight.

- Allows the homeowner to stay in the home while accessing a portion of the home's equity, using the home as collateral.

- No monthly mortgage payments are required. However, the homeowner must live in the home as their primary residence, continue to pay required property taxes, homeowners insurance, and maintain the home according to Federal Housing Administration requirements. Failure to meet these requirements can trigger a loan default that may result in foreclosure.

- The homeowner receives payments on flexible terms as a lump sum, tenure, term, or line of credit.

- A reverse mortgage cannot get "upside down," so the heirs will never have to repay more than the home's value.

- Heirs inherit the home and keep any remaining equity after the reverse mortgage balance is paid off.

- Loan proceeds are not taxed as income or otherwise (though you must continue to pay required property taxes).

- The interest rate may be lower than traditional mortgages and home equity loans.

Assuming that you have gone through your own calculations and have a solid knowledge of your financial situation, it is now time to assess your risk profile.

CHAPTER THREE

RISK

It is vital that you feel confident investing, so you need to recognize and evaluate your risk tolerance for this to happen. In addition, it will be vital in developing a strategy that meets your objectives.

Your Tolerance For Risk

What is risk tolerance? — Simply put, risk tolerance is the level of risk an investor is willing to take. Being able to gauge your risk appetite accurately can be tricky. Risk is about tolerating the potential for losses, the ability to withstand market swings, and the inability to predict what's ahead.

Behavioral scientists say "loss aversion" can play a more significant role in decision-making than the anticipation of gains and can color your approach to risk. Since your comfort level with uncertainty determines risk tolerance, you may not become aware of your appetite for risk until faced with a potential loss.

Risk tolerance vs. Risk Capacity

Though similar in name, your risk capacity and risk tolerance are generally independent of each other. Your risk capacity, or how much investment risk you can take, is determined by your financial situation.

Unlike risk tolerance, which is a measure of how much risk you can withstand emotionally and might not change over the course of your life, risk capacity is more flexible. It depends on how much risk you can handle financially. It varies depending on your personal and financial goals and your timeline for achieving them.

Your time horizon depends on what you're saving for, when you expect to begin withdrawing the money and how long you need that money to last. Goals like saving for college or retirement have longer time horizons than saving for a vacation or a down payment on a house.

When you accurately gauge your limits for investment risk and then invest in a portfolio that reflects your risk tolerance, time horizon, and personal circumstances, you're one step closer to achieving your financial goals.

If you misjudge your risk tolerance or go against what you know to be true about yourself, problems will arise. For example, many investors make the mistake of thinking they are aggressive when they are moderate. Then, when the stock portion of their portfolio takes a drastic fall in price, they sell the stocks right away, even if their previously gauged risk tolerance suggests they would do nothing during a severe decline in prices.

Domain-Specific Risk - When evaluating risk, you need to be specific to the activity or domain. For instance, one may take a chance to parachute or bungee jump but be very conservative with their investments.

Know yourself. If you tend to be easily bored, that trait can be hazardous to your stock market health. The stock market is not the place to get a thrill or act on impulses by taking on high-risk investments.

In any case, check yourself out by taking the following free online evaluation tools, which are specific to the investment risk domain. ***Doing this should be at the top of your priority list before you go to the next chapter.*** I recommend that you take the free "Investment Risk Tolerance Quiz" at https://www.ifa.com/ and the "investment Risk Tolerance Assessment" at https://pfp.missouri.edu.

CHAPTER FOUR

TYPES OF RISKS

Risk-On and Risk-off - Investors' appetite for risk rises and falls over time. Stocks are generally considered to be riskier than bonds. Therefore, a market where stocks are outperforming bonds is said to be a risk-on environment. Conversely, when stocks sell off and investors run for shelter to bonds or gold, the environment is risk-off. Risk-on is usually characterized by expanding corporate earnings, an optimistic economic outlook, an accommodative central bank, and speculation. A stock market rising relates to a risk-on environment, while a drop in the stock market equates to a risk-off environment. It is essential not to get shaken out of your long-term strategy during risk-on and risk-off volatility periods. Therefore, having a disciplined asset allocation model based on your risk tolerance is essential. There is no way to eliminate risks when investing, only mitigation through diversification. Some of the risks that can affect your portfolio are:

Headlines – Headline risk is the possibility that a news story will adversely affect the value of an investment. It can also influence a specific sector or the entire market.

A typical example is the case of an acquisition announcement. When one company acquires another, the stock prices of both companies tend to move in opposite directions. The acquired company's stock rises because the acquiring company is willing to pay a premium for the acquisition, providing an incentive for the acquired company's shareholders to approve the takeover.

In the internet age, negative news can affect a stock's price almost instantaneously, especially with the rise of electronic and high-frequency trading. For example, on October 29, 2020, the price of Twitter dropped 20% on a single trading day due to a news report of slower-than-expected growth. Likewise, during COVID-19, discovering a new variant in South Africa caused the Dow to drop almost 1000 points overnight.

The best thing to do in these situations is to relax. These are almost always just knee-jerk reactions for traders to react on.

Interest Rate – Interest rate risk is the potential that a rise in overall interest rates will reduce the value of a bond or other fixed-rate investment. As interest rates rise, bond prices fall, and vice versa. This means the market value of existing bonds drops to offset the more attractive rates of new bond issues.

Rising interest rates can also negatively affect the stock price of companies with a large amount of debt on their balance sheet. They can also affect growth company stocks with high valuations as the market tends to swing from growth to value stocks.

Geographic – is the risk that an investment's returns could suffer due to political changes or instability in a country. Take, for example, China. They have become the source of production for much of our economy, mainly because of their low labor costs. So when supply chain delays from China occurred during COVID, our economy felt the effect. The same is true of Vietnam, a significant source of clothing. In addition, since many integrated circuit chips are made overseas, a potential economic and national security problem could occur if disrupted by political instability in Taiwan, a critical source of semiconductor manufacturing.

Inflation - is the risk that the future value of an investment, asset, or income stream will be reduced, especially true of companies with high infrastructure costs and debt on their balance sheets.

The concept of Supply and Demand is a key factor when talking about inflation. In essence, the law of Supply and Demand describes how the price of an item tends to increase when the supply of that item decreases (making it rarer) or when the demand increases (making the item more sought after). Conversely, it describes how items will decline in price when they become more widely available (less rare) or less popular among consumers.

Supply chain problems exacerbate the inflation situation. At this writing, the U.S. ports are a bottleneck for goods coming from overseas, notably China and Vietnam. In addition, shipping containers are piling up on ships offshore and on the docks because of the lack of labor to offload and truckers to deliver.

During inflationary times, some companies that dominate a market have the luxury of price elasticity and can raise prices to keep earning good profits, while others in more highly competitive industries do not have that status. Hence, their stock price may suffer because their earnings will decline.

"Wealth Effect" demand – The wealth effect is a behavioral economic theory that suggests consumer spending increases as their overall wealth rises via stocks and assets. The idea is that when a person's investment portfolio or home increases in value, they feel more confident and spend a lot higher and faster, even if income and monthly costs remain the same.

Earnings Reports – Stocks can also suffer reductions in price because of a poor quarterly earnings report, unmet analysts' expectations, or a weak future outlook by the company.

Economic Reports – Many other numbers can affect the market, such as the Consumer Price Index (CPI). The monthly announcement of this index indicates the percent change since the previous month of the market basket of goods and services tracked by the CPI. Since it shows the direction of prices, it is considered an indicator of inflation.

The CPI only scratches the economy's surface, while the Producer Price Index (PPI) gives us a more profound and broader look into the economy. It looks at inflation from the point of view of businesses, measuring prices received from sellers.

PPI tracks prices paid higher up in the supply chain, measuring costs paid by businesses for components, materials, and services that go into the products and services they sell to consumers and other companies. This "intermediate demand" is where you get a glimpse of the accurate scale of the inflationary pressures in the economy.

Political - Politics can potentially impact the stock market somewhat because political actions like regulation and laws affect companies, and thus their actual performance.

In addition, presidents appoint economic advisors and fill positions such as the chair of the Federal Reserve, who determines short-term interest rates.

Uncertainty regarding political decision-making that is currently in process may cause stocks to trade sideways because potential investors don't know whether the final decisions will be positive for business, harmful, or neutral.

Systemic Or Stock Market Risk - Systemic risk is the risk of loss due to the factors that affect an entire market or asset class. It is also known as undiversifiable risk because it affects all asset classes and is unpredictable.

Stock Market Corrections - Periodically, the market will go through a correction or sizable downturn in the order of 10%, which is considered a moderate decline. More significant market downturns can happen quickly and will affect most stocks like an outgoing tide affects all boats. Once they happen, the crowd may panic sell, but you need

to *take a deep breath and stay put because you have the liquidity to ride out the storm if you followed the advice in the first chapter.*

Signs Of A Stock Market Bubble:

- Stock prices are rising rapidly out of proportion to their companies' fundamental value (earnings, assets, etc.)

- Euphoria – caution is thrown to the winds during this phase as asset prices skyrocket.

- Panic – A minor event can prick the bubble, causing prices to reverse course, resulting in margin calls; panicking investors and speculators to liquidate their holdings at any price.

Some of the most memorable include the dot-com bubble in 1999 and the 2008 real estate bubble. During the '90s, the excitement around the internet ran high, and any company remotely having "internet" in its name rocketed, even though it had no earnings or viable long-term prospects. A few prospered, like Google and Amazon, but most companies collapsed.

The 2008 financial crisis was due to excessive monetary stimulus and a flood of demand for real estate. In addition, the administration at the time was encouraging banks to make dubious mortgage loans to people who could not repay them. These bad loans were bundled and sold to institutional investors like insurance companies, pension funds, and banks. When the loans started going wrong, the entire financial system became stressed. Suddenly, the music stopped, and there weren't any chairs left for retail investors to sit on. The bubble popped, a massive sell-off began, and the great recession set in.

CHAPTER FIVE

BUILDING YOUR PORTFOLIO

"You must trust yourself more than you trust others. Pay attention to your inner voice—it will tell you if how and in what you are investing is right for you." - Suzy Orman

---

How much you should invest each month to become a millionaire by age 65

According to Brian Stivers of Stivers Financial Services, the three most important elements of investing are the amount you contribute each month, the rate of return, and how long you have to reach your goal. So when doing the math, Stivers accounted for three different return rates and used a retirement age of 65,

When making calculations, Stivers accounted for return rates: 3% (a conservative portfolio of mostly bonds, 6% (a combination of stocks and bonds), and 9% (a portfolio that's stock-heavy or contains index or mutual funds yielding around 9% on average). And, he used a retirement age of 65,

30-year-old – Calculations would give 30-year-olds 35 years to reach $1 million. Here's the breakdown:

- A 30-year-old making investments that yield a 3% yearly return would have to invest $1,400 per month for 35 years to reach $1 million.

- If they instead contribute to investments that give a 6% yearly return, they would have to invest $740 per month for 35 years to end up with $1 million.

- But if they choose investments that yield a 9% yearly return, which is comparably more aggressive, they would need to invest $370 per month for 35 years to reach $1 million.

    Compared to those who begin investing at age 25, people closer to age 30 will have to contribute a little more money each month to reach the same goal by age 65. Of course, compound interest is most powerful when it has a longer amount of time to grow your money but, still, it's never too late to start investing — even if you don't think you have enough money to invest $370 per month dutifully.

45-year-old — Calculations would give 45-year-olds just 20 years to save. Here's how much 45-year-olds would need to invest each month to become a millionaire by the traditional retirement age:

- If making investments that yield a 3% yearly return, a 45-year-old would have to invest $3,100 per month to reach $1 million by age 65.

- If they instead contribute to investments that give a 6% yearly return, they would have to invest $2,200 per month for 20 years to end up with $1 million.

- But if they choose investments that yield a 9% yearly return, which is comparably more aggressive, they would need to invest $1,600 per month for 20 years to reach $1 million.

If you were to start investing for a 9% yearly return just five years earlier at age 40, you would need to contribute $950 per month to reach $1 million by age 65.

Investment Possibilities

"Buy what you know" was the mantra of Peter Lynch, the charismatic Fidelity Magellan Fund manager from 1977 to 1990.

He preached it like gospel and argued that amateur investors have an advantage that professional investors rarely use, namely, "the power of common knowledge.... During a lifetime of shopping, you have a sense of what is good and what is bad, what sells and what does not."

You might ask, where do I start with all the investment possibilities available? You can begin with your knowledge about the products you like and the companies that make them. Next, think about the items you frequently buy and the stores where you shop. For instance, if you are thinking of buying a retail company's stock, walk into that store and check out the atmosphere, the people traffic, the floor displays, and the courtesy of the employees. Happy employees are one mark of good management.

Great managers often find new business opportunities in unexpected places. So if a company has a strong record of entering and profitably expanding new lines of business, make sure to consider this when valuing a company's stock you are thinking of buying.

One example is Facebook starting in 2004 on the Harvard campus to keep track of friends and what they were doing in their lives. The founders then realized that they could allow free usage but still make money by judiciously placing targeted ads using data-gathering on the people using Facebook. In a short period of time, Facebook has gone viral with millions of users. In 2012 it went public at $30 a share, and now it's a multi-billion dollar company.

Reflect for a moment on how you would typically check out the best quality for the price when shopping for any big-ticket item. Likewise, you need to approach buying stock in a company with the same attitude. That means you have to do your homework using the vast source of corporate information on the internet.

You may not have a graduate degree in technology, but it is evident that technology is changing the world and will continue to do so. For example, the smartphone is essential for anything we need to do, bringing a world of knowledge to our fingertips.

There are many investment opportunities. Choose the ones you feel comfortable with (retail, health, energy, etc.). You don't need perfect vision to pick companies with a solid track record producing products that people will want.

Once you have a solid financial foundation, know your risk tolerance and the stock market risks you may face in the future, then explore the various investment assets you can choose on your way to financial freedom. First are the investment vehicles that may appeal to the low-risk-tolerant investor. Naturally, they would be those having a high degree of diversification built into their structure.

Mutual Funds - A mutual fund is a professionally managed investment fund that pools money from investors to purchase securities, such as stocks and bonds. Each share represents an investor's part ownership in the fund and its income.

Some characteristics of a Mutual Fund to look for:

Low Fees or Expenses - Mutual funds with relatively low expense ratios are always desirable, and low expenses do not mean low performance. In fact, it is often the case that the best-performing funds in a given category are among those that offer expense ratios below the category average. Some funds charge substantially higher-than-average fees and justify the higher fees by pointing to the fund's performance. But the truth is there is very little genuine justification for any mutual fund having an expense ratio much over 1%. In addition to the basic operating expenses charged by all funds, some funds charge a "load," or a sales fee that can run as high as 6% to 8%, and some charge fees used to cover advertising and promotional expenses. There is no need for mutual fund investors to pay these additional fees since there are plenty of excellent funds to choose from that are "no-load" funds and do not charge any additional fees.

Consistently Good Performance - Investors should select a fund based on its long-term performance, not because it had one great year. Consistent performance by the fund's manager, or managers, over a long period of time indicates the fund will likely pay off well for an investor in the long run.

A thought that comes to mind is a quote about fund managers from Jason Zweig, noted investment writer for The Wall Street Journal. " Finally, once a fund becomes successful, its managers tend to become timid and imitative. As a fund grows, its fees become more lucrative—making its managers reluctant to rock the boat. The very risks that the managers took to generate their initial high returns could now drive investors away– and jeopardize all that fat fee income. So the biggest funds resemble a herd of identical and overfed sheep, all moving in lockstep."

Sticking to a Solid Strategy - The best-performing funds perform well because they are directed by a sound investment strategy. Therefore, investors should be aware of the fund's investment objective and the strategy the fund manager uses to achieve that objective.

Trustworthy, With Solid Reputations - The best funds are perennially developed by well-established, trustworthy names in the mutual fund business, such as Fidelity, T. Rowe Price, and the Vanguard Group. With all the unfortunate investing scandals over the past 20 years, investors are well-advised to do business only with firms in which they have the utmost confidence regarding honesty and fiscal responsibility. Therefore, the best mutual funds are invariably offered by companies that are transparent and upfront about their fees and operations, and that do not try to hide information from potential investors or in any way mislead them.

Index Funds -

Index funds are investments made up of stocks that mirror the companies of a market index, such as the S&P 500, which contains 500 of the largest publicly traded companies listed on stock exchanges in the United States. Another example, the Russell 2000 index, includes the 2000 smallest companies out of the 3000 publicly traded companies incorporated in the United States.

Index funds are passively managed and have lower fees than actively managed funds like mutual funds and often generate higher investment returns. In addition, index funds are well-diversified investments. The index fund also eliminates the risks of individual stocks and market sectors. As a result, only stock market systemic risk remains.

John Bogle, Vanguard Group founder and proponent of the index fund, says, "Don't look for the needle in the haystack, just buy the haystack."

Exchange-Traded Funds (ETFs) - Another alternative to mutual funds is the exchange-traded fund, a basket of securities that you can buy or sell during the trading day through a brokerage firm on a stock exchange as you would a stock.

ETFs are offered on virtually every asset class (stocks, fixed income, cash, infrastructure, commodities). Market ETFs track a particular index fund like the S&P 500 or NASDAQ. Bond ETFs provide exposure to U.S. Treasury, corporate, municipal, international, high-yield, and other interest-bearing instruments.

Sector and industry ETFs provide exposure to a particular sector, such as oil, pharmaceuticals, technology, etc.

ETFs are more transparent than mutual funds, mainly because ETFs have a "culture of transparency." Every ETF issuer posts the daily holdings for their funds on free, publicly available websites. On the other hand, mutual funds are only required to disclose their holdings quarterly.

By and large, ETFs also tend to be lower in cost than mutual funds as they charge lower operational expenses. This means you will typically pay less to invest in ETFs than you would in comparable mutual funds over the long haul.

ETFs simply employ better technology. ETFs require less record-keeping and fewer employees to remain operational so that ETF providers can pass the cost savings onto you.

ETFs are also more tax efficient. Mutual funds are pools of investors that are treated as one account holder. This means you pay tax on your share of the pool's capital gain that year, even if you didn't make a single transaction.

Stocks

Individual stocks are of interest to those investors who are willing to take on more risk.

Stocks are simply units of ownership in a company. You are purchasing a partial ownership stake in a company, entitling you to certain benefits. Therefore, understanding stocks and how they work is one of the keys to investing.

Stocks are bought and sold on "stock exchanges." The dominant exchanges in the U.S. are the New York Stock Exchange (NYSE) and the NASDAQ. The NYSE, in general, lists mostly mature companies while technology companies tend to list on the NASDAQ.

NYSE companies are usually identified by a unique symbol like K for Kellogg Company, F for Ford Motor Company, KO for Coca-Cola Company. The NASDAQ uses mostly four-letter characters (tickers) like AAPL for Apple, NFLX for Netflix, and MSFT for Microsoft.

CHAPTER SIX

STRATEGIES

"Investing is a business where you can look silly for a long period of time before you are proven right"
- Bill Ackman

Investing is both a science and an art – the science of fundamental and technical analysis and the art of using your vision and intuition.

An investment strategy is a way of thinking that shapes how you select your portfolio investments. The best strategies should help you meet your financial goals and grow your wealth while maintaining a comfortable level of risk that lets you sleep at night. There are two paths to take, a more passive strategy for the beginning investor or a more active one for the more experienced investor.

The beginner would most likely set up a permanent portfolio that requires little attention but also generates very little excitement.

The active path would be more intellectually challenging, requiring real-time research and monitoring. Many people would feel comfortable in combining a little of both. It depends on your available time and your temperament.

I recommend taking a diversified approach for the beginning stock market investor by investing in ETFs. They are an affordable way to invest in many stocks, bonds, or other assets; and give you diversification and professional money management. They are traded on exchanges like the NASDAQ and the New York Stock Exchange (NYSE).

There is now overwhelming evidence that attempting to predict which securities will outperform and when is a losing strategy for the vast majority of investors. Moreover, even the most skilled fund managers can rarely do this with any long-term consistency.

The alternative to attempting to beat the market is by investing in ETFs using a Buy and Hold strategy. First, choose a diversified asset mix that maximizes your expected return for your chosen level of risk. Then continue to buy ETFs in line with your asset allocation, using dollar-cost averaging to ensure that you buy more shares when markets are down and profit when they bounce back up. Reinvest all dividends to leverage compound interest and rebalance periodically to manage your risk.

Ignore market upheaval and never commit the cardinal sin of locking in losses by selling when your assets are down. Don't churn assets and rack up trading costs by constantly chasing the next 'hot' asset class or fund. Investors are rewarded for taking a risk over the long term, so sit tight during volatile periods. By investing in low-cost ETFs, you can diversify conveniently and cheaply and ensure that you hold on to long-term market returns.

Warren Buffet gave his seal of approval to Buy and Hold when he said: "Our favorite holding period is forever." Meanwhile, German investing legend André Kostolany described the effect of over-trading on investors when he commented, "Back and forth makes pockets empty."

Exchange-Traded Fund (ETF) Strategy - ETFs are an affordable way to invest in many stocks, bonds, or other assets. In addition, they give you diversification and professional money management.

Investing in a multi-asset ETF, which includes stocks, bonds, or real estate, allows you to get the most return for the amount of risk you are willing to take.

Another strategy is to invest in basic index ETFs that match the returns of a financial index, such as the S&P 500 or the Bloomberg Barclays U.S. bond index.

There are sector ETFs that invest in different industries, from e-commerce to energy. The following XLY ETF illustrates a typical holding list.

The XLY ETF, Consumer Discretionary SPDR Fund Top 10 Holdings (11/1/21)

Top 10 Holdings	% Assets
Amazon.com Inc	22.51
Tesla Inc	14.24
Home Depot Inc	8.71

Nike Inc	4.62
McDonald's Corp	4.51
Lowe's Companies Inc	3.67
Starbucks Corp	3.52
Target Corp	3.11
Booking Holdings Inc	2.40
TJX Companies Inc	2.23

Some other sector and index ETFs are:
IVV - iShares Core S&P 500
SKYY- First Trust Cloud Computing
XLF-Financial Select Sector
VGT-Vanguard Information Technology Index
ESPO -Vaneck Video Gaming & Esport
VPU-Vanguard Utilities Index
VHT-Vanguard Health Care Index
XLE-Energy Select Sector
XLC -Communication Services Sector
There were 2,567 ETFs on the market as of June 30, 2021, with almost $6.58 trillion of assets under management.

Individual Stock Strategy – Ultimately, we decide to purchase any investment that we believe will increase in value over time. Selecting a stock investment is no different. However, the value of a stock is ultimately tied to the profits generated by the underlying company. Therefore, investors who believe that a company will grow its earnings in the long run or think it is undervalued may be willing to pay a higher price.

Stock market behavior at any time is the cumulative effect of individual decisions based not only on rational reasons like earnings, the economy, expectations *but also too often on the emotions of fear and greed. Experienced investors ignore these periodic market tantrums because they know that the underlying business fundamentals will determine long-term price trends.*

So why do stock prices change? The best answer is nobody knows for sure. Some believe that it isn't possible to predict how stocks will vary in price, while others think you can determine when to buy and sell by drawing charts and looking at price movements. The only thing we do know as a certainty is that stocks are volatile and can change prices rapidly.

Nevertheless, higher demand for a stock relative to the supply can drive the stock price higher, so the question is, what causes that increased demand in the first place? Ultimately, demand for a stock is driven by how confident investors are about that stock's prospects.

In the short term, things like quarterly earnings reports that beat expectations, analyst upgrades, and other positive business development can lead investors to be willing to pay a higher price to acquire shares.

On the flip side, disappointing reports, analyst downgrades, and adverse business developments can cause investors to lose interest, thus reducing demand and forcing sellers to accept lower prices.

Sometimes the demand for stocks in general increases. A broad-based demand increase can drive individual stocks higher without any company-specific news. One example, the COVID-19 pandemic, led to consumers spending online at the expense of brick-and-mortar stores.

Key Fundamental Questions - Don't forget that money invested in the stock market should be for the long term, and therefore, with that in mind, you need to ask the right questions before buying a stock:

- What does the company do? Warren Buffet famously says he doesn't invest in what he doesn't understand. You need to know how it makes money—what are its products and services?

- Is the company profitable? Look at the data from many angles, especially historical profit margins and earnings results. What is the outlook for the future?

- How rich is the company's valuation? price to earnings ratio (P/E) is one indicator. (see terminology in the appendix).

- Who are its competitors? Does it have the most significant market share, or is it a small but growing niche player in a competitive industry?

- Who is running the show? Buying a stock is like going into business with the management. Their website should list top management and give some insight into the company's history. If the company's executive suite has a rotating door, beware!

- How clean is the balance sheet? A considerable amount of debt and significant inventory levels should be a concern.

- What are the biggest threats to the industry and the company?

- What fundamental changes would cause you to sell it?

Wide Moat Companies — Some "wide moat" companies have businesses with sustainable competitive advantages. Think of a moat around a castle – the wider the moat, the harder it is to breach. One type of wide-moat company is one that is a low-cost producer due to a better business model. The second type is when a company owns a powerful product franchise or brand that consumers are willing to pay more. Some recent examples are Bank of America (NYSE: BAC), BlackRock (NYSE: BLK), eBay (NASDAQ: EBAY), Kellogg (NYSE: K), Lockheed Martin (NYSE: LMT), Nvidia (NASDAQ: NVDA)

The Trading Day

Because many trader's orders begin to execute as soon as the markets open at 9:30 EST, contributing to price volatility, it's best to read the market without making moves for the first 15 to 20 minutes. The middle hours are usually less volatile, and then movement picks up again toward the closing bell at 4 PM EST.

Decide on the type of orders you will use to enter and exit trades. For example, will you use a market or limit order? When you place a market order, it's executed at the best price available at the time, thus no price guarantee. A limit order guarantees the price but not the execution. Limit orders help you trade with more precision, wherein you set your price for buying and selling. But, of course, if no one is willing to buy or sell at the limit price you set, the trade just won't happen.

When you check your holdings, you might see a reasonably significant increase or decrease during the day. Some numbers may seem substantial, but it's not the change in the price of a stock but the percentage change that will tell you whether to look further into the cause or not. If the market is up significantly and your holding is down, that would be a reason to check why, whether it is a temporary glitch or something more serious, an earnings miss, perhaps.

We all hate to see losses in a stock, and there is a temptation to buy more of it, trying to lessen the loss by averaging down. However, continuing this strategy can lead to a downward spiral and result in sending good money after bad. On the other hand, if you own a stock and it keeps going up steadily with good fundamentals, consider buying more, especially if it's in a leading sector.

Usually, if a stock has been treading water for some time, it may decrease in price because the market will soon lose patience and sell it. But if you believe in its fundamentals for the long term, you may want to stick with it.

Stay cool. There are times when the stock market tests your nerves, so learn to keep greed and fear at bay. ***Decisions should be governed by logic, not emotion.***

The U.S. Government will want a cut of your profits. Remember that you will have to pay taxes on short-term gains on any investments you hold for one year or less at the marginal rate.

Seasonal Effects - The stock market has a seasonality that could affect your trading days. September has historically been the weakest month. Average returns in June and August have also been negative. This has led to the expression, "Sell in May and go away." This doesn't mean you should sell your portfolio and go to cash. Still, it does point to being cautious with your portfolio during the summer months when traders and investors are on vacation, resulting in lower liquidity and higher volatility.

Understanding the "Santa Claus Rally" – A Santa Claus rally is a seasonal phenomenon, according to The Stock Trader's Almanac, a longtime provider of analysis of both cyclical and seasonal market tendencies. According to the 2016 edition of the Almanac, "since 1969, the Santa Claus rally has yielded positive returns in 34 of the past 45 holiday seasons—the last five trading days of the year and the first two trading days after New Year's. The average cumulative return over these days is 1.4%, and returns are positive in each of the seven days of the rally, on average."

Related is the "January effect," which is the tendency of small stocks to produce significant gains right after the new year. First, this effect is caused by many investors selling their worst-performing stocks late in the year to lock in losses that can cut down on their tax bills. Second, professional managers grow more cautious as the year draws to a close, seeking to preserve their outperformance or minimize their underperformance. When the tax-driven selling ceases in January, these stocks tend to bounce back and can produce a robust and rapid gain.

CHAPTER SEVEN

ACTIVE INVESTING

"The stock market is a giant distraction from the business of investing." - John C. Bogle

An active investing strategy involves the investor's ongoing buying and selling activity by continuously monitoring and exploiting profitable conditions.

Growth Investing - Growth investors prefer trading more frequently to capitalize on new opportunities, such as buying shares of emerging companies poised to grow at an above-average pace in the future. Companies like this often offer a unique product or service that competitors can't easily duplicate.

The FAANG stocks fit this category: Facebook (renamed META), Apple, Amazon, Netflix, and Google. They have a commanding lead in their sectors by recognizing early on the advantages of using the online capabilities of the internet. Recall that Jeff Bezos of Amazon started as an online bookseller competing with Barnes and Noble, but now note the dominance of Amazon not only in books but in all of e-commerce.

At one point, it looked like Microsoft was going to crush Apple, but then came the iPhone, which has changed our lives. In addition, search engines like Google allow access to the world's information in seconds. Netflix started in 1997 purely as a movie rental service and has grown to become one of the world's leading internet entertainment platforms.

The latest change is coming to the banking industry with the emergence of Fin-Tech, financial technology companies, offering all kinds of services without having the expense of brick and mortar locations. Instead, the internet is a virtual location allowing employees to work online remotely worldwide.

Value Investing - Value investors are bargain shoppers. They seek stocks believed to be undervalued, not fully reflecting the security's intrinsic value. If you are a true value investor, you believe in buying the business and not just the stock, so typically you will be in it for the long run. Warren Buffet is the epitome of a value investor.

Several sites have helpful value stock screeners: Yahoo Finance, Investorplace.com, www.fool.com, fortunebuilders.com. Some value stocks at the current time are Berkshire Hathaway, Procter & Gamble, and Johnson & Johnson.

Income Investing - Income investing is a wealth-building strategy that involves assembling a portfolio of assets that generate dependable cash payouts. For most investors, that would mean a collection of dividend-paying stocks and high-quality bonds that can be counted on as a source of cash requiring little, if any, extra work or input from the investor. Typically those who choose income investing are high net worth investors whose goal is low-risk capital preservation with an income stream to finance their everyday lifestyle.

The first component of this strategy is a dividend-paying stock portfolio. A dividend is the distribution of a company's earnings as a token reward to a class of its stockholders. Most profits are usually kept within the company as retained earnings, used for ongoing and future business activities. The remainder can be allocated to the shareholders as dividends. Larger and more established companies with more predictable profits are often the best dividend payers. New and other high-growth companies, such as technology companies, would likely not offer a dividend but instead, use earnings for future growth.

Dividend payments impact the share price, which may rise on the announcement approximately by the amount of the dividend declared and then decline by a similar amount at the opening session of the ex-dividend date because anyone buying the stock on that date will not receive the dividend.

Some examples of solid companies and their dividend yields are: (11/2/21)

Lowe's (NYSE:LOW)	1.37%
Walgreens Boots Alliance (NYSE:WBA)	4.00%
Realty Income (NYSE:O)	3.93%
Johnson & Johnson (NYSE:JNJ)	2.56%
Target (NYSE:TGT)	1.38%

The second consideration is the bond component. One vehicle is to invest in bond index funds, which pay interest monthly instead of individual bonds, which pay semi-annually. Bond index funds can also have a growth component. Unfortunately, most bond investments do poorly in a rising interest rate environment except if using a passive bond strategy.

The passive buy-and-hold bond investor is typically looking to maximize the income-generating properties of bonds. The premise of this strategy is that bonds are assumed to be safe, predictable sources of income. Buy and hold involves purchasing individual bonds and holding them to maturity. Cash flows from the bonds can be used to fund external income needs or can be reinvested in the portfolio into other bonds or other asset classes.

Momentum Investing – Momentum investing is based on the premise that recent performance continues. So, instead of buying low and selling high, you keep what increases in value and sell assets that do not perform. The philosophy is that proven trends will continue; therefore, putting more money into high-performing stocks will likely bring positive returns.

Momentum investing can be complex, employing technical analysis signals that dictate specific market entry and exit points. It also involves observing moving averages and the relative strength of securities. Short selling, as well as buying strategies, are necessary tools.

It also has an inherent risk because when more investors follow suit, the same momentum can dislocate asset prices from their fair value and cause dramatic price reversals. Therefore, momentum investing should be treated as a short-term high-performing strategy. ***This method of investing is probably more accurately called trading for a short-term return and not investing for the long run.***

Sector Rotation

Sector rotation is another active investing strategy by moving money invested in stocks from one industry to another as investors and traders anticipate the next stage of the economic cycle. As a result, they move their money into sectors that tend to perform best in the next cycle. Let's explore the economic and stock market cycles and how they are related.

The Economic Cycle in Four Stages

Full Recession – This is not a good time for businesses or job-seekers. Gross domestic product (GDP) is retracting quarter-over-quarter. Interest rates are falling. Consumer expectations have hit bottom. Sectors that have historically profited most in this stage include:

- Cyclicals and transports (near the beginning)
- Technology
- Industrials (near the end)

Early Recovery – Things are starting to pick up. Consumer expectations are rising. Industrial production is growing. Interest rates have bottomed. Historically, successful sectors at this stage include:

- Industrials (near the beginning)
- Basic materials
- Energy (near the end)

Late Recovery – Interest rates may be rising rapidly, and the yield curve is flattening. Consumer expectations are beginning to decline, and industrial production is flat. Historically profitable sectors in this stage include:

- Energy (near the beginning)
- Consumer staples
- Services (near the end)

Early Recession – The overall economy looks bad. Consumer expectations are at their worst. Industrial production is falling. Interest rates are at their highest. Historically, the following sectors have found favor during these challenging times:

- Services (near the beginning)

- Utilities

- Cyclicals and transports (near the end)

The Stock Market Cycle in Four Stages

The stock markets don't move with the economic cycle. Instead, they move in anticipation of the economic cycle or try to. The market cycle can be divided into four stages:

- Market bottom: A long-term low point is reached.

- Bull market: The market rallies from the market bottom.

- Market top: The bull market starts to flatten out.

- Bear market: Here we go down again. This is the precursor to the next market bottom.

Most of the time, financial markets attempt to predict the state of the economy anywhere from three to six months into the future. That means the market cycle is usually well ahead of the economic cycle. This is crucial for investors to remember because the market will always start to look ahead to recovery while the economy is in the pits of a recession,

The preferred method of sector rotation investing is through exchange-traded funds or ETFs. These funds have favorable characteristics that make it simple to flow through different sectors given their liquidity, low costs, and low barriers of entry.

When the economic cycle changes, investors using rotation would allocate their assets across different sectors. Therefore, asset allocation is one of the fundamental factors you need to consider when sector investing.

Sector Investing Risks
Buying and selling stocks using a sector rotation strategy can be tricky, so every investor must consider the risks when moving in and out of different sectors.

There could be the risk that the stock you are trading out of performs better than those you are trading into, so it's essential to understand what you're buying at the stock and sector level.

Market timing is another risk. The timing of sector rotation can be difficult to pinpoint for investors. An easy solution to market timing risk is simply sticking to a long-term investment plan. Construct a portfolio that allows you to benefit from different themes or trends in the marketplace but doesn't expose you to all the risks.

The Bottom Line – Sector rotation is a popular way to pursue an active investing strategy by rotating in and out of sectors based on what's happening in the economy. Using mutual funds and ETFs, sector rotation can be a relatively easy way for the average investor to take a more tactical approach to investing and potentially capture higher returns. In addition, this strategy can be combined with the portfolio rebalancing you may already be doing to make sure you maintain your desired level of investing risk.

Sector rotation doesn't make sense for all investors, though. That's because this type of investment strategy requires you to make more frequent investment decisions than you would with a traditional buy-and-hold approach. It also may increase the overall risk and volatility in your portfolio, and it could introduce transaction costs and taxes you might otherwise avoid.

While the goal of executing sector rotation is to achieve higher returns than the overall market, the risk of mistiming your rotation decisions could mean that you end up underperforming broad market benchmarks. That's why most experts recommend people who aren't professional investors stick with passive, index-based investing.

CHAPTER EIGHT

PASSIVE INVESTING

The essence of passive investing is a long-term approach in which investors don't trade much. Instead, they purchase and then hang onto a diversified portfolio of assets usually based on a broad, market-weighted index, like the S&P 500 or the Dow Jones Industrial Average. The goal is to replicate the financial index performance overall — to match, not beat, the market.

Perhaps the most common passive investing approach is to buy an index fund tied to the market. These sorts of funds are often known as passively managed or passive funds. The underlying holdings in passive funds can be stocks, bonds, or other assets — whatever makes up the index being tracked. If the index replaces some of the companies included in it, the index fund automatically adjusts its holdings, selling the old stocks and purchasing the new ones. Thus, investors profit by staying the course and benefiting from the market increases that happen over time. Typically, index funds specialize in such areas as equities, fixed income, commodities, currencies, or real estate. Choosing different funds depends on the investor's desire for income or growth, risk tolerance, and needs to balance the portfolio.

Some of the key benefits of passive investing are:

- Ultra-low fees – oversight is much less expensive.

- Transparency – always clear which assets are in the fund.

- Tax efficiency – does not result in large capital gains.

- Simplicity – does not require constant research and adjustment.

Index investing is one common strategy whereby investors purchase a representative benchmark, such as the S&P 500 index and hold it over a long-term horizon.

Index fund managers generally believe it is difficult to out-think the market, so they try to match market or sector performance by constructing well-diversified portfolios of single stocks, which would require extensive research if done individually. ETFs that track major indices simplified the process further by allowing investors to trade index funds as though they were stocks.

Dollar-cost averaging (DCA) is employed to mitigate market volatility risk. It's the process of investing the same dollar amount in a specific asset over regular time intervals regardless of the asset's price. So, when the market goes down, your cash buys more shares, and you buy fewer shares when the market goes up. You may be doing DCA right now without knowing it.

For example, you are already using DCA if you have a 401 (k) or similar plan where you automatically invest a percentage of every paycheck in a retirement plan. That's because every pay period, you are investing the same amount of cash like clockwork.

But while systematic investing does not guarantee a profit or protect you from loss, it can lift a psychological weight off your shoulders. With DCA, you don't need to agonize over whether you should buy right now or wait for earnings or a market dip. Instead, you just implement the system and keep yourself updated periodically.

Buy & Hold - A list of top buy-and-hold practitioners is a who's-who of the greatest investors of all time: Warren Buffett, Jack Bogle, John Templeton, Peter Lynch, and Warren Buffett's mentor Benjamin Graham.

If you put your money into the SPY (S&P 500) exchange-traded fund (ETF) and forgot about it over a period of time, you would have beaten 75% of actively managed fund managers. The biggest drawback is that your money is tied up for a long time, and you need to have the discipline to leave it alone through a bear and bull market.

Still, buy-and-hold remains one of the most popular and proven ways to invest in the stock market. The practitioners of this strategy do not have to worry about timing the market or basing their decisions on subjective technical analysis patterns.

Notwithstanding the benefits of this strategy, you should not blindly hold any asset. You still have to act prudently to guard against market crashes and know when to cut losses and take profits.

Nevertheless, if you believe in the economy and the stock market's future, these are just a few of the companies that have withstood the test of time and could be part of a buy-and-hold portfolio:

Advertising: Facebook, Google
Insurance: Berkshire Hathaway
Consumer Products: Kimberly-Clark, Procter & Gamble
Retail: Walmart, Target, Costco
Wireless Communications: Verizon, AT&T, T-Mobile
Soda Production: Coca-Cola, Pepsi

CHAPTER NINE

DIVERSIFICATION AND ALLOCATION

"The beauty of diversification is it's about as close as you can get to a free lunch in investing." - Barry Ritholtz

---

Your portfolio generally should be diversified to minimize the risk of putting all your eggs in one basket. You may have mutual funds or ETFs, and that is fine, but make sure the holdings are diversified enough so that if a sector of the industry falls off a cliff, your financial security doesn't go with it. The same is true of your stock holdings.

Technology is considered a sector but is not as homogeneous as many other sectors like autos, banking, real estate, health care, renewable energy, etc. The ongoing technology revolution is transforming all sectors. Think of how critical semiconductor chips are to phones, self-driving cars and how they make it possible to perform instantaneous searches on the internet. Today's smartphone has so much technology embedded in it that it would have required a large room in the 1950s. Technology has made gaming more and more realistic and will be vital in developing the metaverse.

I consider Cathie Wood of Ark Funds a visionary, and I agree with her about the future of technology. "In five years, the world will look nothing like it looks today, and we are invested in all the disruptors, the winners, that are going to disrupt the traditional world order." To put numbers to Wood's theory, she said that innovation is currently priced at roughly between $10 trillion and $15 trillion in the global public marketplace. In 10 years, disruptive innovation will be about $200 trillion of that market capitalization. "It will go from a little bit more than 10% of global equity market cap to what we believe could be more than half," said Wood. "That's how much disruption is evolving thanks to DNA sequencing, robotics, energy storage, artificial intelligence, and blockchain technology."

One current example is in the field of surgery. Oculus headset technology supplied by META (Facebook) is already being used at UConn Health, the University of Connecticut's medical center in Farmington, Connecticut, to train orthopedic surgery residents. Educators have teamed with PrecisionOS, a Canadian medical software company that offers VR training and educational modules in orthopedics. Donning Oculus Quest headsets, the residents can visualize in 3-D performing a range of surgical procedures, such as putting a pin in a broken bone. Because the procedure is conducted virtually, the system allows the students to make mistakes and receive feedback from faculty to incorporate on their next try.

"Good, bad or indifferent, if you are not investing in new technology, you are going to be left behind," - Phillip Green

---

This bundle of ETFs is presented in order to analyze the impact of technology within a diversification bundle. But, first, let's check out the results in this snapshot taken on 11/22/2021.

The ETFs (with their top two holdings)	Annual % return
XLY Consumer Discretionary Sector SPDR Fund	37.22
Tesla 20%	
Amazon 20%	
XLF Financial Select Sector SPDR Fund	45.58
Berkshire Hathaway 12%	
JP Morgan Chase 12%	
SKYY First Trust Cloud Computing ETF	30.23
DigitalOcean Holdings 5%	
Rackspace Technology 4%	
ESPO VanEck Video Gaming and eSports ETF	16.29
Nvidia 9%	
Advanced Micro Devices 8%	
VPU Vanguard Utilities Index Fund ETF Shares	7.02
Nextera Energy 15%	
Duke Energy 7%	

VHT Vanguard Health Care Index Fund ETF Shares	19.49
Johnson & Johnson 7%	
Unitedhealth Group 6%	
VNQ Vanguard Real Estate Index Fund ETF Shares	28.68
Vanguard Real Estate II Index Fund 12%	
American Tower 7%	
XLE Energy Select Sector SPDR Fund	55.38
ExxonMobil 23	
Chevron 20%	
XLC Communication Services Select Sector SPDR Fund	23.23
Meta Platforms 21%	
Alphabet Class A 13%	

One of the financial XLFs core holdings is Warren Buffett's Berkshire Hathaway, whose most significant position by far is $130 Billion (with a B) of Apple stock. Apple is Hathaway's "third-largest business" after its wholly-owned insurance and railroad businesses. Buffett has described the technology giant Apple as "probably the best business I know in the world."

The average yearly return for this entire ETF bundle works out to 29.23%, a very nice return on investment. Note that many of the holdings are technology-oriented, which will continue to do well over time.

I also tracked the IVV iShares Core S&P 500 ETF, and its return was a little better at 31.62%. Finally, the VGT Vanguard Information Technology Index Fund yielded a 38.657% return.

Of course, all these numbers could change in any given yearly period, but experience indicates that they wouldn't vary very much. **_Hence, the takeaway is that a technology fund as a core holding along with an S&P 500 Index fund might be two excellent choices to have in your portfolio._** With that being said, your vision, common sense, and fundamental analysis are still essential when making investment decisions.

Allocation - There are no easy answers to allocation because investors have a wide range of investment goals, risk tolerance, and behavioral characteristics. However, there are two fundamental factors on allocating: *your ability* to take risks and *your willingness* to take risks. The first is dependent on your financial situation, and the second is dependent on your ability to weather the market's ups and downs without worry.

Age and Allocation - Jason Zweig disagrees with those proponents who base allocation strictly on age, i.e., the older you are, the less risk you should take and put all your eggs 100% into bonds. Zeig responds: " Why should your age determine how much risk you should take? For example,

> an 89-year-old with $3 million, a generous pension, and a gaggle of grandchildren would be foolish to move most of her money into bonds. She already has plenty of income, and her grandchildren (who will eventually inherit her stocks) have decades

of investing ahead of them. On the other hand, a 25-year-old saving for his wedding and a house down payment would be foolish to put all his money in stocks. Then, if the stock portfolio takes an Alcapulco high dive, he will have no bond income to cover his downside." The lesson is that we all have different circumstances, so forget all the pundits and use your common sense.

Let's examine some portfolio allocation models:

- **A conservative portfolio** would allocate a large percentage to fixed income and money market securities. The primary purpose is to protect the principal and is referred to as a capital preservation portfolio.

- **A moderately conservative portfolio** is for those who wish to preserve most of the portfolio's total value but are willing to take some risk for inflation protection. Investment choices would be securities that pay high dividends or coupon payments.

- **A moderately aggressive portfolio** is a balanced composition between fixed-income securities and equities and is suitable for investors with a longer time horizon.

- **An aggressive portfolio** mainly consists of equities to achieve long-term capital growth. In addition, some diversification is obtained by adding fixed-income securities.

- **A very aggressive portfolio** consists entirely of stocks with the goal of capital growth over a very long time horizon.

Bottom line: Neither diversification nor asset allocation can ensure a profit or protect against a loss. There is no guarantee that a diversified portfolio will enhance overall returns or outperform a non-diversified portfolio.

Portfolio Rebalance -

You built your portfolio's allocation mix based on your goals, time horizon, and risk tolerance. But goals can change, and market fluctuations can cause your asset allocation to shift, so it's essential to monitor your portfolio regularly and make adjustments as needed. For example, Vanguard recommends checking your asset allocation every six months and making adjustments if it's shifted five percentage points or more from its allocation target.

Minimize transaction fees and taxes - When it's time to rebalance your portfolio, consider tax-efficient practices to potentially further improve your investment performance without sacrificing your risk/return profile. For example, selling investments from a taxable account that's gained value will most likely mean you'll owe taxes on the realized gains. To avoid this, you could rebalance within your tax-advantaged accounts only.

Manage risk and emotion - Every investor's dream is to buy low and sell high. But the purpose of rebalancing is to manage risk, not maximize returns. Rebalancing isn't about market timing—it's about sticking to a strategy to stay in sync with your long-term goals. Since bull and bear markets don't last forever, it's important to remove yourself from difficult decisions by sticking to a fixed rebalancing strategy. It's a way to take your emotions out of investing, keep your allocation in check, and limit the higher taxes associated with frequent rebalancing.

CHAPTER TEN

WORDS TO THE WISE

"Experience is a dear teacher, but fools will learn to no other." - Benjamin Franklin (1706-1790)

This chapter is a cautionary one, dealing with avoiding the pitfalls of high-risk, get rich quick investing strategies, especially for those investors without in-depth market experience.

Initial Public Offering -An initial public offering (IPO) refers to the process of offering shares of a private corporation to the public in a new stock issuance, thereby raising capital. Companies must meet the requirements of the Securities and Exchange Commission (SEC) to hold an IPO. In addition, companies hire investment banks to market, gauge demand, set the IPO price, date, and more. ***Be careful about investing in new stock issues (IPOs) when they first list on the stock market.*** Prices usually immediately spike up and then can drop dramatically. It takes time for new issues to settle down. If the stock has staying power, there will be plenty of time to profit from it. Even Facebook spiked upon initial trading and then dropped, presenting a much safer buying opportunity later.

SPAC Investing -
A SPAC is a special purpose acquisition company (also known as a blank check company) formed to raise money through an initial public offering to buy another company. At the time of their IPOs, SPACS have no existing business operations or even stated targets for acquisition. When you buy a SPAC, you essentially give your money to the SPAC's founder, or sponsor, without knowing exactly how the sponsor will invest it. The sponsor may be an individual or group. Sometimes the sponsor will specify a target industry. While in other cases, the sponsor has free rein. Much of the appeal comes from the retail investors' ability to get in on the ground floor, to buy SPACs at or near the initial price. SPACS have two years to complete an acquisition of a private company, or they must return their funds to the investors.

SPAC Risks:
- Inadequate management due diligence – There may be a rush to buy firms that aren't suited for public markets to meet the two-year deadline.

- Inaccurate financial reporting because company statements are not reviewed by the SEC.

- Material misstatements and omissions – A SPAC faces minimal scrutiny about its operations, unlike an IPO.

- Inadequate controls – SPACs may invest in hot sectors that may be short-term fads instead of viable long-term businesses.

- Conflicts of interest – sponsors may have fiduciary obligations to other entities that compete with the SPAC's business.

Speculation - There can be the temptation to get rich quickly by investing in a sure thing, maybe someone's suggestion or the latest fad. Keep a cool head and do your due diligence before investing. *But if you want to speculate, put aside a small amount in a "fun" account, never to be added to, and get the exciting part of your investing out of your system.*

Margin - I put margin in the temptation category. "My buddy at work just got a hot tip, and I want to go for broke (no pun intended), but I don't have all the funds that I want to invest in my cash account, so I'll take a loan from my broker and buy on margin."

Don't even think about it. Margin is, in fact, another form of speculation!!
Buying on margin occurs when an investor buys an asset (stock) by borrowing from a broker. Buying on margin refers to the initial payment made to a broker for the asset—for example, 10% down and 90% financed. A margin call from a broker is usually an indicator that one or more of the securities held in the margin account has decreased in value. When a margin call occurs, the investors must either deposit more money or sell some of the assets held in their account to cover the call. ***A broker can legally sell all or part of your holdings to cover the call without your permission.***

Timing - Timing the market includes actively buying and selling to try and get into the market at the most advantageous times while avoiding disastrous times. Unfortunately, this is only a pipe dream for the vast majority of investors. ***The most likely outcome is that "timers" wind up following the crowd by buying high and selling low.***

Day Trading - Day trading is the practice of purchasing and selling within a single trading day. Day traders are typically well-educated and well-funded. ***This is a seriously intense business—a full-time job, not a hobby.***

Options - These are conditional contracts that allow buyers of the contracts (option holders) to buy or sell a security at a chosen price in the future. Investing in this arena requires extensive knowledge of multiple option strategies found in many books on the subject. Briefly, when investors trade options, they can choose between a call option or a put option. The investor speculates that the underlying stock's price will rise in a call option. Conversely, a put option takes a bearish position, where the investor bets that the underlying stock's price will decline. Options are purchased as contracts, equal to 100 shares of the underlying stock.

Meme Stocks - Meme stocks refer to stocks that have gone viral with internet popularity, whose only value is rooted in social sentiment rather than solely on core economics or corporate indicators. They are touted on a forum called Reddit's Wall-StreetBets. From Game Stop to AMC Entertainment, the 11 million-member forum has driven the conversation in so-called meme stocks that have exploded higher amid overwhelming demand from retail investors. Memes have the potential for monumental gains and significant losses because of rapidly volatile price changes. When large numbers of retail investors band together, the price swings can be dramatic. Meme stocks are also a symbol of market democratization—some call trading in these stocks entertainment trading, akin to gambling.

You might be sympathetic with the meme craze cause, but stay clear!

Short Selling - In short selling, an investor borrows a stock from a lender (broker), hoping the stock will go down in price. If the stock does drop after selling, the short seller buys it back at a lower price and returns it to the lender, making a profit on the difference. ***There is no limit to losses if the stock keeps going up. This is a sure way to lose sleep.***

Personally, if I had the power, I would ban short selling. Unfortunately, many hedge funds used this tactic to pile on AMC Theaters. Many of these hedge funds lost billions when the meme investors consolidated their buying of AMC stock to drive the price up, forcing the hedge funds to sell at a considerable loss.

Falling In Love With A Stock - Not all stocks are winners. Sometimes you have to cut your losses, even though you thought you had a sure thing. Be patient if a stock you bought has dropped, but the fundamentals are still fine. On the other hand, if you observe deteriorating financials over time, you should ask yourself, *Would I buy it today?* If not, then maybe it's time to sell it.

Sky Rockets - Don't chase a skyrocketing stock. ***What goes up quickly can also fall just as quickly, without warning.*** This cycle is typical during the first few days of an IPO.

Surprises - Sell companies that come up with negative surprises. *If you see one cockroach, there are probably more lurking in the cupboard.*

Penny Stocks - Penny stocks trade at very low prices, sometimes at less than a dollar a share, and are bought and sold over the counter and not on a major exchange. Any stock that does not trade on the NYSE, NASDAQ, or other established U.S. exchange can trade over-the-counter.

They are highly risky because companies that list OTC aren't required to file periodic or audited financial reports, as they must do if listed on a major exchange. So you have no idea if their sale and profit information is confirmed. The other problem is that they tend to be illiquid and can make it difficult or impossible to buy or sell shares at the price an investor wants. *The bottom line is that you could lose your total investment. Stay clear!*

Cryptocurrency

Cryptocurrency is all the rage now, but remember it's still in its infancy, so be prepared for ups and downs and dramatic swings in prices. As a result, it's not an investment I would recommend as there is no intrinsic value, and fundamental analysis is not possible. Instead, ***it is purely a speculative play.*** When you own bitcoin, you don't own a piece of a company. Instead, you make money in one way–by selling it to somebody else for more money than you bought it for – sounds like a Ponzi scheme?

Cryptocurrency is a payment system that doesn't rely on banks to verify transactions. Instead, it's a peer-to-peer system that can enable anyone to send and receive payments. Instead of being physical money carried around and exchanged in the real world, cryptocurrency payments exist purely as digital entries to an online database that describes specific transactions. When you transfer cryptocurrency funds, the transactions are recorded in a public ledger, and you store your cryptocurrency in a digital wallet. Even though there is no intrinsic value nor an ability to perform fundamental analysis, crypto, bitcoin, and ethereum, are probably here to stay.

CHAPTER ELEVEN

YOUR ADVISOR

"Investing is not nearly as difficult as it looks. Successful investing involves doing a few things right and avoiding serious mistakes" - John C, Bogle

---

When choosing an advisor, it's essential to decide whether you want to be a hands-on DIY investor or prefer to take a passive approach by using a full-service brokerage to manage your investment account for you. A full-service broker may be suited for investors who are not familiar with what they should be investing in, don't want to spend the time to research or manage their investments or have a large amount of wealth that requires complex financial management.

Investors who choose the DIY approach, and prefer a low-cost way to manage their assets, may select an online brokerage account or discount broker that enables them to buy and sell investment securities through the broker's website or app.

I recommend a full-service brokerage for the beginning investor, with a qualified advisor to help you if needed. Popular brokerages are Charles Schwab, Fidelity, Etrade, and Raymond James. Be aware that fees can be quite high depending on the services you need.

Large Brokerage Houses - When choosing a brokerage, consider the kind of services available such as financial planning, consulting, trust services, and wealth management, and whether they have branch offices near you.

Full-service brokerages tend to have service fees for managing your account. For example, they may charge a flat fee or a percentage of your assets under management. They may also charge commissions on trades.

Advice from any quarter is always a mixed bag. However, most brokerages have an analytical department that answers inquiries and can make recommendations. Brokerages have confined themselves to executing orders given to them, supplying financial information and analysis, and rendering opinions on the investment merits of securities. Thus, in theory, they are devoid of responsibility for their customers' profits or losses.

Small Investment Firms - These firms usually have fully credentialed advisors, who in many cases worked for a big firm, and then started on their own. Many of these smaller firms will require a minimum of a $300,000 investment and probably will take a very safe strategy by investing your money 50% in bonds and 50% in dividend-paying stocks. But, again, this is not necessarily a bad practice. Still, I would consider it a low-risk approach for them to provide a better investment return than the S&P 500 index while reducing their firm's liability.

Independent Registered Investment Advisors - This area has a wide range of competence and honesty, so proceed cautiously. Make an appointment and ensure that the advisor has met all SEC and state requirements; that you feel comfortable during the interview. Please be discerning. As Ronald Reagan used to say, *"Trust, then verify."*

Above all else, trust your advisor enough to permit them to protect you from your worst enemy—yourself. "You hire an advisor," explains commentator Nick Murray," not to manage money, but to manage you."

You Can Do It Yourself - If you take the time to study the basics, investing is not difficult, and you may soon feel confident, becoming your own advisor saving money in the process. Become a critical thinker and don't take Wall Street "fact" for granted. Instead, invest with patience, develop discipline and courage, and refuse to let another person's passion affect your financial decisions. Then, when you are experienced, confident, and feel comfortable, I recommend that you use a DIY approach by logging on and using a brokerage's website or app to make changes to your portfolio. If you use this method, make sure the website is intuitive and easy to use. The benefits will be instant access to your entire portfolio and zero commissions for trades.

A Robo-Advisor – provides a low-cost alternative to hiring a human investment manager: These companies use sophisticated computer algorithms to choose and manage your investments for you, based on your goals and investing timeline. Robo-advisors are likely a good fit for you if you'd like to be largely hands-off when it comes to your investments.

Fintech – Fintech is financial technology. Fintech products are designed to make it easy to connect a consumer's finances with technology. From insurance and investment companies to mobile payment apps, fintech is a game-changer that poses a risk to traditional banking and financial institutions. Financial technology offers many applications that focus on the consumer, providing resources that change the way consumers access, manage, and track their finances. Most importantly, fintech is reaching 2 billion people globally without bank accounts so that they can access financial services without the need for traditional financial institutions. A prime example is Robinhood.

The Robinhood Phenomenon

Robinhood is a fintech online investing platform offering commission-free trading of stocks, options, ETFs, and cryptocurrency. It is very popular with young investors who seem to have a mission to democratize the stock market. You can buy fractional shares and use margin (not advised). You also have access to initial public offering investments. You can simply download the app and set up an account quickly. It is best for active traders and day traders who want to purchase and sell stocks frequently with no commission.

Robinhood and Fidelity offer commission-free trading, but you will have a broader range of investments with a brokerage like Fidelity than you will with Robinhood.

CHAPTER TWELVE

YOUR ACCOUNT

A brokerage account is the type of account used to buy and sell securities like stocks, bonds, and mutual funds. You can transfer money into and out of a brokerage account much like a bank account, but unlike banks, brokerage accounts give you access to the stock market and other investments.

Many brokers allow you to open a brokerage account quickly online. However, you will need to fund the account before you purchase investments. You can do that by transferring money from your checking or savings account or another brokerage account. You may also be able to mail in a check.

You own the money and investments in your brokerage account, and you can sell investments at any time. The broker holds your account and acts as an intermediary between you and the investments you want to purchase.

Brokerage accounts vs. retirement accounts

A standard brokerage account, or taxable account, offers no tax advantages for investing through the account — in most cases, your investment earnings will be taxed. On the plus side, that means there are very few rules for these accounts: You can pull your money out at any time, for any reason, and invest as much as you'd like.

But if you're investing for retirement, you'll want to open a retirement account rather than a taxable brokerage account. A retirement account, such as a Roth or traditional IRA, is a tax-advantaged investment account specifically designed for your retirement savings. Because of that, unlike taxable brokerage accounts, retirement accounts place restrictions around when and how you can withdraw the money, as well as how much you can contribute each year.

How to open a brokerage account

Setting up a brokerage account is a simple process — you can typically complete an application online in under 15 minutes. In most states, Once you've opened the investment account, you'll need to initiate a deposit or funds transfer. That sounds complicated, but these days, it's a pretty simple process to link your bank account with a brokerage account and can be done online.

Some brokers may require you to verify a transaction. If that's the case, you'll have to wait until the broker deposits a small sum in your bank account — typically a few cents — and you'll confirm the transaction by letting the brokerage know the exact amount that was deposited. Then, the broker can walk you through the process if you have any questions. After the transfer is complete and your brokerage account is funded, you can begin investing.

You might be asked if you want a cash or margin account. A margin account allows you to borrow money from the broker to make trades, but you'll pay interest, and it's risky. So generally, it's best to stick with a cash account at first.

CHAPTER THIRTEEN

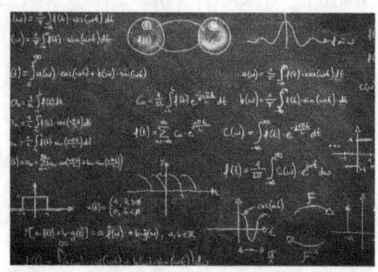

KEEP IT SIMPLE

By keeping it simple and focusing on the long-term horizon, you can ensure your chance of success.

- Invest in what you understand. Diversify in sectors and stocks with which you are comfortable.

- Research the fundamentals.

- Only invest what you can afford to lose.

- Have realistic expectations. The unlikely scenario of doubling your money in a year might only be possible by taking on a lot of risks.

- Be prepared to hold for a long time (expecting a quick return is a folly). Be patient, and keep your focus on a company's actual performance. Stocks tend to be volatile, bouncing around with knee-jerk reactions to headline news. ***Trying to predict the market's short-term movements is impossible.***

- Stay with a winner - ***"If it isn't broken, don't fix it."***

- The trend is your friend. Past performance can be a good indicator of how a company will perform in the future. But you always have to be on the lookout for the trend to change. Disruptive technologies can appear on the scene, as happened with the internet's advent.

- Think independently - ***follow your intuition.*** The crowd is usually wrong. Successful investing is more about temperament than it is about having exceptional intelligence.

- ***Keep cool when everyone else is panicking.*** The stock market can drop sharply at times (called corrections). This is quite normal, but at these times, the media likes to exaggerate with headlines of, "Sell, Sell, Sell!" Maybe this is the opportunity to think of adding to your portfolio.

- Investing in assets is risky, but it tends to work out over time. *"It's time in the market, not timing the market. That is the key to having your assets appreciate."*

CHAPTER FOURTEEN

WISDOM FROM THE WIZARDS

Stock Market Reporting - There is a lot of noise in stock market reporting. You will often hear from short-term traders rather than long-term investors. Traders thrive on volatility, trying to buy on the lows and sell on the highs. Another term bandied about is rotation from one sector to another depending on the latest headline news, like inflation fears causing a rotation out of growth stocks into discretionary stocks. Machine trading algorithms also can affect the market's course instantaneously flowing with the school of what's happening now. As long-term investors, we should instead heed common sense wisdom from some of the giants in the investment industry.

These quotes all tell the same story:

1. Research an equity before investing until you feel confident deep down that it is a good investment.

2. Unless you see something has substantially changed in your investment, stay with it no matter what you hear in the headlines. The headliners always amplify the terrible news.

3. You can expect your investments to decline in value if there is a broad market selloff, but you haven't lost anything unless you sell.

4. Time is your friend so stay long.

"Everyone has the brainpower to make money in stocks. Not everyone has the stomach. If you are prone to selling everything in a panic, you ought to avoid stocks and mutual funds altogether."
- Peter Lynch

"The investor's chief problem, and even his worst enemy, is likely to be himself,"
- Benjamin Graham

"I will tell you how to be rich. Close the doors. Be fearful when others are greedy. Be greedy when others are fearful."
- Warren Buffett

"On investing, what is comfortable is rarely profitable."
- Robert Arnott.

"Courage taught me no matter how bad a crisis gets….any sound investment will eventually pay off."
- Carlos Slim Helu

"The individual investor should act consistently as an investor and not as a speculator."
- Ben Graham

"Know what you own, and know why you own it."
- Peter Lynch

"We don't have to be smarter than the rest. We have to be more disciplined than the rest."
- Warren Buffett

"Successful investing is about managing a risk, not avoiding it."
- Benjamin Graham

"The four most dangerous words in investing are: 'This time it's different.'"
- Sir John Templeton

"In investing, what is comfortable is rarely profitable."
- Robert Arnott

"Every once in a while, the market does something really stupid."
- Jim Cramer

CLOSING CHAPTER

THOUGHTS ABOUT YOUR JOURNEY

It has been my privilege to be your guide throughout this book. You have made some significant preparation on your investment journey.

Remember, the world is constantly changing, so keep your vision sharpened. Be on the lookout for disrupting advancements that will provide investing opportunities. To keep being a winner, you have to always be on top of new developments in the investing world.

Don't be turned off by high financiers and their grand portfolios. Instead, take that first step to achieve what you have conceived, and develop the mindset to be the winner you already are. I wish you the best and happy investing.

Frederick A. Wilhelm Jr.

ACKNOWLEDGEMENTS

Thanks to Christina Wilhelm, Gerry Isaac, and Steve Kalling for their invaluable advice and editing, making this book possible. I also am grateful to pixabay.com for the images.

APPENDICES

Appendix A - Financial Terminology

Beta is a word for volatility. The overall market has a beta of 1. Anything above 1 is more volatile (price movement), and anything below 1 is less volatile, less risky. Utility stocks exhibit low betas.

The **VIX** Index is a 30 day expected volatility of the U.S. stock market, also called the fear index, because a rising number indicates market instability. In contrast, a falling number suggests that traders expect the S&P 500 index to trade more quietly. The VIX was first calculated in 1992. The lowest recorded was 9 on 10/4/2007, and the highest recorded was 82 on 3/16/2020, just before the COVID-19 downturn. A VIX below 12 is considered low, and a Vix above 20 is considered high. Usually, when the Vix rises dramatically, the S&P 500 will drop, signaling a possible buy entry.

Revenue represents the number of sales of goods and services.

Profit Margin is a measure of profitability and indicates how many cents of profit has been generated for each sales dollar. A net profit margin of 10% is considered average.

Earnings refer to the income that a company gains during a specific period usually expressed as earnings per share (EPS). Negative earnings aren't necessarily bad if the profit margin is high. For example, Amazon had negative earnings for years because it reinvested back into the company to ensure future growth.

The price-to-earnings **(P/E)** Ratio is the ratio for measuring a company's current share price relative to its earnings per share. It is also known as the price multiple or earnings multiple. A high P/E ratio could mean that a company's stock is overvalued or that investors expect high growth rates in the future. On the other hand, companies with no earnings or are losing money do not have a P/E ratio because there is no number to put in the denominator.

Appendix B - Stock Analysis 101

Fundamental Vs. Technical Analysis —Technical analysis uses past data of a stock to predict future price movements. Fundamental analysis instead looks at economic and financial factors that influence a business. The first step to technical analysis starts with charts, whereas fundamental analysis starts with the company's financial statements.

In fundamental analysis, you will have to determine its intrinsic value by looking at its income statement, balance sheet, and cash flow statement. The intrinsic value of a stock can be determined by discounting the value of future projected cash flows to the net present value. If the stock trades below the company's intrinsic value, you can invest in it.

The time horizon in fundamental analysis is often long-term, as opposed to a short-term approach taken by technical analysis. This is because technical analysts and fundamental analysts have very different goals in their minds. For example, technical analysis will make many short- to medium-term trades, whereas fundamental analysis look to make long-term investments.

Fundamental Analysis

Fundamental analysis has been one of the most rewarding analyses in the history of stock markets. In fundamental analysis, you evaluate security using economic, financial, qualitative, and quantitative factors to determine its intrinsic value. It is believed that macroeconomic and microeconomic factors can affect a security's value. These factors can be economic, industry, financial, and management proficiency. The main motive while doing a fundamental analysis should be to evaluate a security's intrinsic value and compare it with the current stock price of the security, thus determining if the security is undervalued or overvalued.

How to do Fundamental Analysis of Stocks - You must understand the company you intend to invest in. It will give you further insight into how the company is performing, whether it is making the right decisions towards its future goal, and whether you should hold or sell the stock.

Visiting its website and learning about its management and products is an excellent way to mine such information.

Study the financial reports of the company

Once you understand the company, you should start analyzing its financials such as balance sheet, profit-loss statements, cash flow statements, operating cost, revenue, expenses, etc. Then, you can evaluate its compounded annual growth rate (CAGR), sales and if the net profit has been increasing for the last five years, it can be considered a healthy sign for the company.

Check the debt

Debt is an essential factor that can bring down a company's performance. A security cannot perform well and reward you if it has a considerable debt of its own. Therefore, avoid companies with massive debt. Always try to find a company with a debt:equity ratio of less than one.

Company's competitors

The company you want to invest in must be one of the best among its peers. Try to find a company which is performing better than the other companies. It should have better prospects, upcoming projects, new plants, etc.

Analyze the prospects

Fundamental analysis is most effective when you want to stay invested long term. So invest in those companies whose products will still be useful 15-25 years down the line or show a history of replacing older products with innovations to keep up with the times.

Review all the aspects from time to time

Do not invest in a company and forget about it. Stay updated about the company you have invested in. You should keep updated about all its news and financial performance. Sell the security if there is a problem in the company.

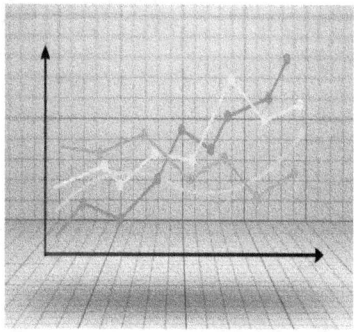

Technical Analysis

Technical analysis is quite similar to the basic principles of economics, such as analyzing supply and demand in the market to determine where the price trend is headed. In technical analysis, you have to evaluate securities by statistically analyzing market data such as price and volume. You use charts and various other tools to understand different patterns. As a technical analyst, you depend on these patterns to help you make investment decisions. You should not be concerned with the stock's valuation but rather about past trading data only.

Fundamental analysts criticize technical analysis because it only considers price movements and ignores fundamental factors such as political impact. However, technical analysts counter this criticism by stating that a stock's price already reflects everything that has or could affect a company. So this removes the need for you to be concerned about fundamental factors. The only thing you should be concerned about is price movement analysis.

Some basic assumptions of technical analysis:

Prices move in trends: Technical analysis assumes that prices move in short, medium, and long-term trends. The stock you pick for analysis will follow the same past trend rather than move randomly.

History tends to repeat itself: Another assumption is that the market history tends to repeat itself. It is believed that the repetitive nature of price movements is due to market psychology. You will have to use chart patterns and historical data to analyze these emotions and understand market trends. While technical analysis has been used for more than 100 years, it is still relevant because stocks follow patterns in price movements that often repeat themselves.

Appendix C - The Federal Reserve

Since 1977, the Federal Open Market Committee (Federal Reserve) has operated under a mandate from Congress to "promote the goals of maximum employment, stable prices, and moderate long term interest rates effectively."

The Federal Reserve Bank of St. Louis publishes extensive economic data, news, and research papers. See online site: fred.stlouisfed.org.

The market is always hanging on every word the Fed is saying, looking for insight about the direction of interest rates. When the interest rate changes, it impacts both the economy and the stock market. The impact of interest rate changes on the stock market is generally experienced immediately, while for the rest of the economy, it may take a year to see any widespread impact.

Since borrowing becomes either more or less expensive for individuals and businesses, it can affect a company's earnings, especially those with debt on their balance sheet.

Growth vs. Value Stock Interest Rate Effects

Stocks are often broken down into value and growth. Value stocks have current solid cash flows that will slow over time, while growth stocks have little or no cash flow today but are expected to increase over time gradually.

Since interest rates are usually increased to combat high inflation, the result is that growth stocks will be more negatively impacted in times of high inflation. This suggests a positive correlation between inflation and the return on value stocks and a negative one for growth stocks like technology.

First, it increases the costs of borrowing more money to expand a business. That's bad news for high-growth tech companies, which are burning cash with widening losses.

Second, it reduces the long-term estimates for a company's earnings and growth. That reduction hurts high-growth companies valued based on their future growth instead of their near-term profits. Therefore, unprofitable tech companies trading at frothy valuations usually suffer the most as interest rates rise.

Lastly, higher interest rates turn bonds into safer investments for big institutional investors. As a result, it's common to see a lot of money rotate from the tech sector into the bond market as yields rise.

Higher interest rate headwinds cause investors to rotate out of tech stocks and toward financial, consumer staples, and industrial companies–which often perform better in a stable economy with elevated interest rates.

It's tempting to follow that trend and avoid tech stocks altogether. However, plenty of resilient tech companies can withstand the inflationary pressure with their pricing power and stable cash flow growth. In addition, some companies have the leverage to negotiate favorable prices with their suppliers and can also raise prices to pass on higher costs to their loyal consumers.

In a high-interest rate environment, you should limit your exposure to tech companies that don't have enough pricing power, lack consistent profits, and trade at high valuations. ***However, stick with the stronger stalwarts and remember that these inflationary headwinds will eventually pass.***

Bond Vigilantes

The term "bond vigilante" usually is attributed to Ed Yardeni, a Wall Street economist who coined it in the 1980s to describe the role of bond markets in disciplining governments. He once declared, "So if the fiscal and monetary authorities won't regulate the economy, the bond investors will." A bond vigilante is a bond market investor who protests against policies considered inflationary by selling bonds, thus increasing yields.

In the bond market, prices move inversely to yields. When investors perceive that inflation risk or credit risk is rising, they demand higher yields to compensate for the added risk. As a result, bond prices fall, and yields rise, which increases the net cost of borrowing. The "Bond Vigilante" term also refers to the ability of the bond market to serve as a restraint on the government's ability to overspend and over-borrow.

Rising Rate effects

- Equity investors can benefit if rates rise at a manageable pace, indicating economic growth.

- Savers benefit with higher rates.

- Bond investors can benefit from a higher interest rate environment, but current bondholders may suffer as bond prices drop to reflect the higher rates.

- Borrowers are at risk, especially those with high credit card debt.

- Businesses and consumers will usually cut back on spending, causing earnings to fall and stock prices to drop.

- Rising rates can also lead to stagflation or the persistent increase in price pressures alongside slowing economic growth.

Lower Rate Effects

In a low rate environment, companies and consumers can borrow cheaply and tend to buy more or invest more, boosting corporate profits, leading to higher aggregate demand and economic growth.

In theory, lower rates will:

- Reduce incentive to save.

- Make the cost of borrowing cheaper.

- Lower mortgage interest payments.

- Make it more attractive to buy assets such as real estate.

Appendix D - Investment News And Research Sources

Knowledge is power. These resources all offer real-time economic and market news and asset analysis to help you be informed as you travel along your investment journey.

CNBC

The one app I particularly like is CNBC. It has a good summary of any stocks you might have in your portfolio. In addition, it offers easy access to news, market indices, portfolio tracking, and features CNBC live audio.

Zacks Investment Research

Zachs is an independent source known for detailed, engagingly written stock and fund picks that go against the grain of conventional wisdom. In addition, the website has an extensive archive of free content for casual investors, including articles, videos, and podcasts covering several topics.

Yahoo! Finance
Yahoo boasts an excellent lineup of complimentary analytic tools, research reports, straight financial news, and user-generated content.

Google Finance
Google Finance is a research site ideal for DIY investors, comfortable performing due diligence with minimal support. In addition, it is free and valuable to keep up with the latest world and U.S. news.

Morningstar
Morningstar has one of the best data sources on mutual funds and ETFs. You can see returns going back ten years and monthly and quarterly returns going back five years. You can find breakdowns of fund holdings, geographic allocations, and much more.

SEC filings
You should go to the SEC filings for in-depth information on a company. There you will find:
   The company 10-K annual report
   10-Q quarterly report
   8-K current event report

The annual director's report and the management discussion and analysis (MD&A) sections are good sources of information on the company and its industry. In addition, there will be information about the management's plans concerning expansion, diversification, technological change, capital, and organizational changes.

www.ingramcontent.com/pod-product-compliance
Lightning Source LLC
LaVergne TN
LVHW011847060526
838200LV00054B/4204